On the Shoulders of Giants: Volume 1. North America

JOSEPH A. WARD

To my good friend
Ms. Leah Aleis I
truly appreciate your
support   J. A. Ward

On the Shoulders of Giants Vol 1: North America

© 2015 by Joseph A. Ward

ISBN # 978-1-329-78974-6

Table of Contents

On the Shoulders of Giants is dedicated to all the persons who gave their lives to freedom and equality, throughout the history of North America. These heroes are the persons who set the stage for us to have the freedoms we have today. We owe it to our ancestors to honor them for their courage, strength, wisdom, beauty and traditions.

"History is not everything, but it is a starting point. History is a clock that people use to tell their political and cultural time of day. It is a compass they use to find themselves on the map of human geography. It tells them where they are, but more importantly, what they must be."
— John Henrik Clarke

"Be as proud of your race today as our fathers were in days of yore. We have beautiful history, and we shall create another in the future that will astonish the world."
— Marcus Garvey

Author's bio

Joseph A. Ward is a certified Life Coach, a graduate of Florida A&M University and holds his Bachelor's degree in Psychology. He possesses over four years of experience in delivering academic success presentations to grades K-12, college-aged students and middle aged adults. By working in diverse venues such as grade schools, college campuses, juvenile divergent programs, correctional Institutions, religious communities, homeless shelters, and foster homes has become skilled at providing valuable life training to a wide variety of community members.

A graduate of the "New Hope Program" with the Florida Department of Health in Leon County, Mr. Ward served as a co-facilitator with the program for over four years, which works to teach life and professional skills to underprivileged persons. He helped to establish the FAMU chapter of MOST (Men of Strength) and currently serves as co-facilitator with the organization. Mr. Ward also successfully developed the Sexual Violence Prevention Program with the Florida Department of Health in Leon County and holds over four years of Sexual/Domestic Violence Prevention training experience with A Call to Men, Men Can Stop Rape, and the Florida Council against Sexual Violence.

Mr. Ward's commitment to his community has proven him to be a reputable teacher, trainer and motivator. He is dedicated to uplifting and educating individuals around the world while helping to create mindsets and environments which foster greatness.

Dedication

On the Shoulders of Giants is dedicated to all the people who gave their lives to freedom and equality throughout the history of North America. These heroes set the stage for us to have the freedoms we have today. We owe it to our ancestors to honor them for their courage, strength, wisdom, beauty and traditions.

"History is not everything, but it is a starting point. History is a clock that people use to tell their political and cultural time of day. It is a compass they use to find themselves on the map of human geography. It tells them where they are, but more importantly, what they must be."

--John Henrik Clarke

"Be as proud of your race today as our fathers were in days of yore. We have beautiful history, and we shall create another in the future that will astonish the world."

-- Marcus Garvey

Introduction

On the Shoulders of Giants is a mini eBook highlighting heroes of African American, African and Indigenous American decent. This eBook is an extension of my blog page On the Shoulders of Giants. This book and the blog page were designed to create awareness about heroes of the past and present who gave the world hope and freedom. It is important to recognize and understand the contributions of those before you, particularly those of African or Indigenous descent. Our past is significant because of the plight we had to overcome and in some aspects are still overcoming, to be considered human beings.

This book is intended to bring awareness and give an alternative perspective of the history of Africans, African-Americans, and Indigenous Americas in North America. I believe the media gives negative perspectives of the history of non-white persons in North America. This book and the volumes to follow will bring light to the major accomplishments of non-whites before, during and after slavery. I feel it is important for the non-white youth of the world to understand the significant impact people of their culture and other cultures have made.

This volume focuses on heroes from Mexico, America and Canada. This book is for the brave trailblazing men and women in history, who used their talents to empower and uplift their people and or fought for their freedom. When one is knowledgeable about their past, their sense of self-worth will improve and they become a vessel of information to pass along to the next generation. The following ten people are trailblazers we can be proud of for serving their people. We stand on their shoulders. Enjoy!!

Chapter: 1

Mathieu Da Costa

Born in the late 1500's, Mathieu Da Costa was a remarkable man. He was a translator who used his skills to become the first person of African descent to reach Canada in recorded history. A Liberian by birth, he was a free African Seaman during the time of the Trans-Atlantic Slave Trade.

Little is known about his life, but we do know, in the early 1600's Da Costa was employed by the French until the Dutch kidnapped him. Da Costa signed a three year contract to work for the Dutch as a translator. He spoke French, Dutch, Portuguese, and Pidgin Basque; a language used in the Americas for trade.

It is still a mystery as to how Da Costa came to learn languages of the Americas, but he used them well to help guide himself, Du Gua de Monts and Samuel de Champlain through Acadia and the St. Lawrence River area. Using the navigation skills he possessed, he was able to lead his employers on expeditions throughout North America during a time when the average African in North America was enslaved. While employed by De Monts, he was able to accumulate some wealth to sustain a decent life until he was imprisoned in December of 1906.

There is no information to show why he was imprisoned, but many suggest that he spoke his mind and was accused of insolence. De Costa was able to use his genius to make a life for himself. He also was a pioneer in reaching the land many enslaved Africans would eventually call home, Canada. Mathieu De Costa, we stand on your shoulders.

Chapter: 2

Gaspar Yanga

Gaspar Yanga was a great man of royal West Africa lineage around the Gabon, Nigeria area. He is said to be a prince who was stolen from his home and placed into the Trans-Atlantic Slave Trade. The word Yanga is said to mean "pride" according to Yoruba traditions. That word describes Yanga perfectly.

Yanga is known as the "first liberator of the Americas." He lead one of Mexico's first successful slave revolts and established one of the first free black settlements in the Americas. Between the years of 1570 and 1609, Yanga managed to escape slavery and began to help others escape leading them into the mountains of Pico de Orizaba, Cofre De Perote, and Zongolica.

By the year 1600, Yanga created a settlement called the Maroon Settlement and was later joined by Francisco De La Matosa along with his own group of African Maroons. This settlement was created before Mexico gained its independence from Spain. As the settlements grew stronger under Yanga's watch, decade's worth of resistance against Spain ensued which lead to a battle between Yanga and Spain's viceroy of New Spain (the name of colonial Mexico) Luis De Velasco, Marquis of Salinas.

In 1609, Velasco sent Captain Pedro Gonzalez on a military expedition against Yanga and his settlements. The height of the battle came at Rio Blanco, which left both sides with tremendous losses to their forces. The battle also made the Viceroy of New Spain respect Yanga.

Rodrigo Pacheco was responsible for negotiating with Yanga, which lead to an agreement and Spain's recognition of the settlement as an African community. The first official name of Yanga's city was San Lorenzo De La Negros, but since 1932, the town's name has changed to Yanga after its founder and liberator. Little is known about his birth or his death, but we do know that Gaspar Yanga stood for freedom at all costs. He risked his life for a future free of enslavement and tyranny.

Yanga was brave and skilled enough to free himself and create a Palenque for his followers to dwell in freedom from the rule of Spain. Gaspar Yanga is an unsung hero in Mexican and American lore, but because of his actions the Africans of Mexico were able to experience freedom. Gaspar Yanga, we stand on your shoulders.

Chapter 3:

Dr. Mae C. Jemison

On October 17, 1956 in Decatur, Alabama, Charlie and Dorothy Jemison welcomed their third child Mae Jemison who would change the world. When Mae was three years old her family moved to Chicago to find better educational opportunities for their children. Early in her school years, Mae was known to spend an enormous amount of time in the school library reading about science, specifically Astronomy.

While attending Morgan Park High School, Mae found her passion. She began pursuing a career in biomedical engineering. Upon graduating from high school in 1973 with consistent honors, she became a student at Stanford University on a National Achievement Scholarship.

Jemison double majored at Stanford receiving bachelor degrees in Chemical Engineering and African American studies in 1977. After graduation, she entered Cornell University pursuing a medical degree. Mae Jemison traveled extensively while at Cornell.

She visited Cuba, Kenya and Thailand, where she worked at a Cambodian refugee camp. She graduated from Cornell in 1981 before attending Los Angeles County/University of Southern California Medical Center where she received hands on training to become a doctor. Using all of her talents and education, Mae Jemison established a general practice.

She later worked as a Peace Corps Officer in Sierra Leone. She used her time there to teach and conduct medical research. In 1985, Mae Jemison returned to the United States and applied for the NASA astronaut training program, but faced a road block when the Space Shuttle Challenger exploded in 1986.

In 1987, she reapplied for the program and was one of fifteen chosen out of a field of two thousand applicants. She was the first African American woman chosen to be a part of the training program. Mae spent more than a year in the training program and became an astronaut, which was accompanied by the title of Science-Mission Specialist.

This title garnered the responsibility of conducting crew-related scientific experiments on the space shuttle. In 1992, Mae Jemison flew into space aboard the Endeavour on mission STS-47. She and her crew spent eight days in space conducting experiments on weightlessness and motion sickness. Mae used herself and the crew as guinea pigs for the experiments.

On September 20, 1992 they returned and Mae became very famous for her achievements as the first African American woman in space. Following her return from space Mae received a plethora of awards and recognitions. In 1998, she received the Essence Science and Technology Award.

In 1990 she was named the Gamma Sigma Gamma Woman of the Year. In 1992, she won the Ebony Black Achievement Award and The Mae C. Jemison Academy was named after her. Between the years of 1990 and 1992, she became a member of the American Medical Association, the American Chemical Society, and the American Association for the Advancement of Science.

She served on the Board of Directors of the World Sickle Cell Foundation. She also became a committee member of the American Express Geography Competition as well as a board member of the center for the Prevention of Childhood Malnutrition. In 1993, she received a Montgomery Fellowship from Dartmouth College.

She also left the astronaut corps to establish the Jemison Group, a company that researches, develops and markets advanced technologies. Mae Jemison became a professor at Dartmouth College and started the Jemison Institute for Advancing Technology in Developing Countries. She later created The Earth We Share program, a science camp for girls ages twelve to sixteen, helping to improve problem solving skills. Mae Jemison is a trailblazer.

She used her imagination to dream of a future that she later made a reality. By becoming the first African-American woman in space, Dr. Jemison opened doors for women of color at NASA forever. Dr. Mae C. Jemison, we stand on your shoulders.

Chapter 4:

José Morelos y Pavon

Jose Maria Telco Morelos y Pavon was born in Morelia, Mexico on September 30, 1765. Born into poverty, he worked as a muleteer and a cowhand from early in life to the age of 25. He was orphaned at the age of fourteen.

When his father left he began working at his uncle's house to make money for his mother. In his spare time he was able to teach himself grammar, Latin and high Spanish. At the age of 25 he began to study for the priesthood at the Colegio de San Nicolas.

He was ordained as a Roman Catholic Priest by the time he was 33. He was born of an interracial relationship between an African and an indigenous American, which helped him gain the trust of the people he was helping. He held several curacies at one time and was able to serve the Indigenous people as well as the mestizos.

In 1810, when Hidalgo was leading the fight against Spain, Pavon approached about his interest in joining the fight. He put together an army in the southern parts of the country to capture the Port of Acapulco, which was a main port of Spanish income. Not long after Pavon joined the fight, Hidalgo was captured and executed by the Royal Spanish family.

Pavon became the successor in the fight against Spain. Because of the brilliance of Pavon, the movement was able to survive Hidalgo's death. Pavon put together an army of indigenous, African and mixed race persons to fight in his army.

Under the control of Pavon, the army gained control over a large piece of land which included the states of Michoacán, Morelos, Puebla, Oaxaca, Guerrero, and Veracruz. The army had its most successful moments under the leadership of Pavon. Using the fame he garnered, he gave a speech in Oaxaca where he vehemently opposed slavery, stating that all human beings are born free and had rights to the lands where they were born.

Pavon later wrote the "Los Sentimientos de la Nacion", (The Feelings of the Nation). It was a declaration that he personally delivered to the National Congress in Chilpancingo in 1813. The greatness of the letter set the foundation for the country's morals and politics. They were created during a tough and trying time for the country.

Congress bestowed Pavon with two distinguished titles, one was "Highness" and the other was "Top General". Pavon, true to the freedom of his people, declined the titles. He was later regarded as a "Servant of the Nation".

In 1814, Pavon and his army were under siege by the Royal forces of Spain at Cuautla. Despite being outnumbered, Pavon was able to break through the Royal Army to put an end to the siege. Suffering only minimal losses to his army, Pavon was able to regroup his forces and take another shot at the Royal Army capturing Oaxaca and Acapulco.

On November 5, 1815 tragedy struck. Pavon was finally defeated by the Royal Army. He was taken to Mexico City as a prisoner and executed by firing squad on December 22nd. After his execution the movement lost its momentum. Pavon's birth city Valladolid was renamed Morelia in 1828.

In 1869, the state of Morelos was created. Because of the influence of an orphaned mixed race ordained priest turned freedom fighter; oppressed people in Mexico were able to live free. Pavon died fighting for what he believed was every human's right, freedom. Mr. Jose Maria Telco Morelos y Pavon, we stand on your shoulders.

Chapter 5:

Bessie Coleman

Bessie Coleman was born January 26, 1892 in Atlanta, Texas to parents Susan and George Coleman. Her parents were sharecroppers so they did not earn a lot of money. In 1901, her father moved to Indian Territory in Oklahoma where he had rights to the land by bloodline. Susan refused to join her husband on the land, so she was left to care for five children by picking cotton, taking in laundry, and ironing for whites.

Susan was a driving force in Bessie's academic life; encouraging her daughter to excel in school despite not having a formal education herself. Bessie missed a lot of school helping her mother in the cotton fields to feed the family. Yet she graduated the eighth grade and attended an industrial college in Oklahoma by saving her money and paying her way.

After dropping out of college, she returned home and helped her mother by washing and drying clothes. By 1915, she moved to Chicago to join two of her brothers who already resided in Chicago. After attending beauty school she worked as a manicurist which helped her meet many influential blacks in Chicago.

Coleman's interest in aviation was piqued by her brothers telling her stories about French women flying planes in World War II. She began reading about aviation and her mind was made up. She tried to enroll in aviation school but was denied on multiple accounts.

She would not give up. A dear friend of Coleman's, Robert S. Abbot, encouraged her to go to France to study Aviation. She got a new job as a manager of a chili restaurant and began studying French at the Berlitz School. In 1920, Coleman left for France and never looked back.

After arriving in France she successfully enrolled into flying school and received her pilot's license, making her the first African American woman to gain a piloting license. In 1921, she returned to the United States and was celebrated by the black press, but was not covered by the white press. She made another trip to Europe and gained training in stunt flying, helping her make a living as a pilot before returning home again in 1922.

Coleman was able to show off those stunt flying skills in an air show on Long Island, New York which was held in honor of black World War I veterans. This air show helped her gain the title of, "The World's Greatest Woman Flyer". She flew in another show in Chicago and gained more fame that eventually spread around the country.

Later Coleman announced her intent to start a flying school for African Americans and began recruiting students for her school. To raise funds she opened a beauty shop in Florida and made more money lecturing at schools and churches. Bessie Coleman's career hit a snag when she was cast to be in a movie. After determining the role to be degrading to her and her morals, she turned down the role.

The decision to stand up for what she believed in caused some of her financial backers to walk away from her. Overcoming the financial setback, Coleman was able to buy her own plane in 1923. It was an Army surplus plane that she would later crash causing her to suffer broken bones.

After an even longer struggle to find financial backers, Coleman was able to find new supporters and book new shows for stunt flying. In 1924, she was able to buy another plane; a low priced older model plane that was more affordable. In April 1926, Bessie Coleman was in Jacksonville, Florida preparing for a May Day Celebration sponsored by the local Negro Welfare League. In preparing for her show, Coleman and her mechanic went out for a test flight.

In this particular flight Coleman was the passenger to her mechanic. Coleman was riding in the plane without a seatbelt in order to get a good view of the ground as she was planning her stunts for the next day. A loose wrench in the plane got wedged in the gear box preventing the control to be used and tragically Coleman was thrown from the plane at 1,000 feet.

The plane subsequently crashed and burned killing her mechanic as well. A memorial for Coleman was held in Jacksonville and her funeral was in Chicago. Both services drew massive crowds of supporters and mourners. In memory of a brave trailblazer, every April 30 African American aviators fly over Coleman's grave and drop flowers.

Both the Bessie Coleman Aero Club and the Bessie Aviators Organization were founded by black women and open to women of all colors in

Bessie's honor. In 1990, a street near the O'Hare International Airport was renamed in honor of Coleman; also the Lambert-St. Louis International Airport unveiled a mural honoring "Black Americans in flight". Bessie Coleman was one of the black Americans included in the mural.

In 1995, Coleman was honored by the U.S. Postal Service with a commemorative stamp. Lastly, in 2002, Coleman was inducted into the National Women's Hall of Fame in New York. Bessie Coleman opened doors for black women in America forever by becoming the first African American woman pilot and perfecting stunt flights. Her tenacity and ability to turn a "no" into a "yes" made her brilliant. Ms. Bessie Coleman, we stand on your shoulders.

Chapter 6:

Reginald F. Lewis

Reginald F. Lewis was born December 7, 1942 in Baltimore, Maryland to parents Clinton and Carolyn Cooper Lewis. Reginald grew up in a section of East Baltimore that was described as a rough neighborhood, which helped shape his approach to life. He had a close relationship with his family, which had a huge influence on his life and his success.

By the age of 10 Lewis began a newspaper route. He grew it from ten customers to over one hundred and then sold it for a profit. Lewis had a knack for business early in life.

Lewis attended school at Oblate Sisters of Providence, a school founded by African American women for teaching African American children. After graduating he attended Dunbar High School where he found himself as the Varsity Quarterback, a Short Stop for the baseball team, and a forward for the basketball team. Lewis developed his leadership skills early as the captain of all three teams and the student body vice president.

After graduating high school, Lewis attended Virginia State University on a football scholarship. Lewis' life took a new direction when he suffered a career ending injury in football. With no sports to play, he turned his tenacity toward his school work and other endeavors. Lewis began working as a sales assistant for a photographer and as always Lewis excelled.

He generated so much business that the owner offered him a partnership. Despite the lucrative opportunity Lewis respectfully declined. It was not in his plans to become a photographer. Lewis had plans of becoming a lawyer and he worked diligently to achieve his goal.

His resolve allowed him to graduate from Virginia State University on the Dean's list. In 1965,

Reginald Lewis learned about a summer program for black legal students at Harvard Law School. He petitioned for his admittance and got accepted. While in the program he took advantage of the opportunity and left a lasting impression on staff members.

In fact, Lewis was so impressive that the Harvard Law School invited him to attend the school in the fall without filling out an application. Lewis is the only person in the history of Harvard Law to be admitted without applying. Lewis' brilliance shined during his time at Harvard. He wrote a thesis during his senior year that earned him an honors grade. In 1968, Lewis graduated from Harvard Law School and began working in corporate law in New York.

Just two years later, Lewis joined with other African American lawyers to create Wall Street's first African-American law firm. Lewis pursued corporate law and became a special counsel to General Foods and Equitable Life. Lewis also became a special counsel to the New York based Commission for Racial Justice during the trial for the Wilmington Ten. Once again, Lewis proved his brilliance and emerged successful when the State of North Carolina was forced to pay the bond of the Wilmington Ten.

In 1983, Lewis founded the TLC Group, L.P. His success began with leveraging a $22.5 million buyout of McCall Pattern Company. The business was struggling when Lewis brought it. Yet he managed the company into two of its most profitable seasons in 113 years. In 1987, he sold the company for $65 million making a 90 to 1 return on his investment.

In August of 1987, Lewis brought the International Division of Beatrice Foods, a corporation that owned 64 companies in 31 countries. Lewis closed the deal on the sale with the help of investment banker Drexel Burnham Lambert and bond king Michael Robert Milken. Lewis rebranded the corporation as TLC Beatrice International and the corporation was valued at $985 million, making it the largest offshore leveraged buyout ever by an American company. Under Lewis' lead the corporation was able to pay down debt and increase the wealth of the corporation. TLC Beatrice International garnered revenues of $1.5 billion making it a fortune 500 company and number one on Black Enterprise top 100 lists.

In January of 1993, Lewis suddenly died of a cerebral hemorrhage. It is rumored in some reports that his death was part of a conspiracy. Before Lewis died he wanted to create a museum for African American culture and in 2002 his dream was realized. The Maryland State Legislature allocated thirty-two million dollars to the building of a museum of African American culture and history. Lewis was a person that relished in the opportunity to become great. He became the first African American to become a billionaire. He left a legacy of excellence and genius. Lewis' success is a result of hard work, dedication and principle. Mr. Reginald F. Lewis, we stand on your shoulders.

Chapter 7:

Jovita Idár

Jovita Idár was born in 1885 in Laredo, Texas to a family in which journalism was the chosen profession. Her father was the publisher of a Spanish newspaper called La Cronica. The newspaper covered issues such as politics, school segregation in the south, poverty, and the preservation of Mexican culture. Idar's brothers started working for the newspaper in their teen years, while Jovita embarked on a career as a teacher helping to combat social injustice at the grass root level.

She became a certified teacher at the age of 17 graduating from the Holding Institute. Shortly after, she began teaching in the city of Los Ojuelos. It was hard for Idár to ignore the issues of racism in Texas; so she began to incorporate political activism in her arsenal. The tragic murder of Antonio Gomez, a 14 year old boy in Laredo in 1911, helped propel Idár deeper into the civil rights struggle of South Texas.

Gomez was being thrown out of a grocery store and was arrested and charged with attempted murder. Gomez was later taken from the jail by a racist lynch mob and beaten to death.

The main culprits in the murder were the Texas Rangers, making the murder a headline in Texas. La Cronica covered and publicized the protest against the Texas Ranger's role in the murder. Idar's father, Nicasio organized the first Mexican Congress, which was created to launch a formal Civil Rights Campaign.

Inspired by the number of women who showed support of her father's efforts, Jovita Idár organized La Liga Feminil Mexicanista (Mexican Feminine League). La Liga helped provide free bilingual literacy classes for Mexican migrant workers, developed a bilingual public school curriculum and opened an Elementary School with new equipment and new learning conditions. La Liga operated strictly by their mission to help empower the Mexican migrant population.

They often allowed poor migrant women to be on their advisory board despite disapproval from their funders Orden Caballeros de Honor. The women of La Liga decided not to buckle under the pressure of their funders, so they cut ties with Orden Caballeros de Honor and started putting on plays to raise funds for their community work. In 1913, The Battle of Nuevo Laredo ensued just across the Rio Grande near Jovita's home.

La Liga changed its focus briefly to help the influx of fleeing families from the Mexican Revolution. La Liga collected food and clothes for the families. They also went into Nueva Laredo to treat casualties of the war. The women helped wounded persons ranging from Civilians to Government Soldiers. The women learned that the U.S. Government played both sides of the revolution and kept U.S. business going while the revolution was happening.

Later in 1913, Idár returned to Laredo and began working for El Progresso, a Spanish language newspaper that was known for criticizing the U.S. Government for interfering with the Mexican Revolution. As a writer of El Progresso, Idár openly criticized President Woodrow Wilson for sending troops to the revolution. She gave eye witness accounts of the behavior of the troops publishing her most controversial article in 1914.

Idár covered a non-violent confrontation between US and Mexican solders over drums of oil from Tampico oil fields. The US soldiers were arrested and held then released following a written apology from the commander of the Mexican forces. Idár accused President Wilson of using the oil event as an excuse to occupy the oil fields in Veracruz and the port of the city.

Days after criticizing Wilson in her publication, Texas Rangers in support of Wilson moved in close to the El Progresso print shop. Idár stood in the doorway of the shop refusing to let any Ranger enter. The rangers later returned with sledgehammers and wrecked the shop and all of its equipment. The attack was severe and the shop never recovered.

In 1914, Nicasio Jovita's father died and his death gave Idár and the staff an opportunity to rebuild the publication. Idár became the editor in chief of La Cronica and was joined by some of the employees of El Progresso. They began to organize unions for the migrant and railroad workers in conjunction with the American Federation of Labor. La Cronica also covered rights issues associated with disgruntled migrant workers.

In 1917, Idár married Bartolo Juarez and moved to San Antonio where she provided a free bilingual school for the children of San Antonio. She spent time volunteering as an interpreter at charity hospitals. She also found time to establish Texas' first Democratic Party-Affiliated political group for Mexican Americans.

Later in her years Idár often wrote for other newspapers in the South Texas region. She wrote editorials on the state of Texas public education and she often wrote against lynching in the Spanish and English Texas newspapers. She was able to write for La Voce de la Patria and La Voce Italiana, where she called for the banding together of immigrant communities against violence against Italian communities during World War II.

Jovita Idár died In San Antonio, Texas in 1945. But not before she was able to donate her personal papers as well as her brother's papers to the University of Texas. Idar's collection was destroyed by a fire in 1965, diminishing her legacy. Yet despite the destroying of her documents, Jovita Idár will live forever in the pages of history.

She gave her life to the freedom and equality of her people and others. She faced the US Government and the Texas Rangers without fear. Jovita Idár was interested in educating the youth so that the culture of her people could survive and be passed on to the next generation. Miss Jovita Idár, we stand on your shoulders.

Chapter 8:

Nathaniel Dett

R. Nathaniel Dett was born October 11, 1882 in Drummondville, Ontario, Canada. His parents were Charlotte Washington Dett, a Canadian, and Robert T. Dett, an American. The grandson of former slaves from Washington D.C. and Maryland, Dett was gifted from a young age. Dett listened to his two older brothers take piano lessons and managed to learn to play the piano by ear. After the piano teacher noticed Dett's talent, she began giving him free lessons at the age of five.

In 1893, his family moved to Niagara Falls, New York where he began taking lessons from John Weiss. By 1901, he studied with Oliver Willis Halstead who was the owner of a conservatory in Lockport, New York. Three years after studying under Halstead he was admitted to the Oberlin Conservatory where he majored in piano and composition.

Four years later, Dett graduated from the Conservatory with a B.M. in Piano and Composition and also won Phi Beta Kappa honors. Dett later studied at Harvard under Arthur Foote as well as the American Conservatory in Fontainebleau under Nadia Boulanger. He later received a Master of Music at the Eastman School of Music in Rochester, New York. In 1911 he released *Album of a Heart* which contained 30 poems.

Dett began working at the Hampton Institute in Hampton, Virginia in 1913. He became the director of the 40-Voice Hampton Singers and set a new standard of excellence for the Hampton Music Department. The 40-Voice Singers performed at Carnegie Hall in 1914.

Also in 1914, Dett debuted what would eventually become his most frequently performed piece, *Listen to the Lambs*. 1919 was a year when *Somebody's Knocking at Your Door* and *I'm So Glad Troubles Don't Last Always* debuted. Dett's *Don't Be a Weary*

Traveler won the Francis Boot prize at Harvard University in 1920.

In 1926, Dett became the Director of the Music Department at Hampton, becoming the first black person to hold that title. Later in 1926, he was awarded an honorary Doctorate of music degree from the Oberlin Conservatory, also making him the first black person to be awarded that honor. On December 17, 1926 the 80-Voice Hampton Choir performed by invitation at the Library of Congress in Washington, D.C.

Their program was a trademark mix of Dett's work which included, early English music, Russian Liturgy, Christmas Carols and Negro Spirituals. Dett conducted a 1928 performance of Tchaikovsky's The Legend in Carnegie Hall. Dett brought spirituals to a new light and to a new audience.

Nathaniel Dett was a musical genius, a leader and a visionary. He was able to infuse black culture into his music and mainstream America loved it. Nathaniel broke barriers in the musical world in a time when racism was openly displayed. Mr. Nathaniel Dett, we stand on your shoulders.

Chapter 9:

Catherine Hughes

Catherine Elizabeth Hughes was born April 22, 1947 in Omaha, Nebraska to parents William and Helen Woods. Catherine grew up in a low income housing project, but her family did not foster a low income mindset. Her father, William, was the first African American to receive a degree in accounting from Creighton University. Her mother was a member of the orchestra at Piney Woods School, a privately owned boarding school Hughes' father funded.

When Hughes was eight years old, her mother gave her a transistor radio and it was then when she found her passion. She would lock herself in her bathroom and use a tooth brush as a microphone having fun dreaming of her future as a media mogul. At age 16 Hughes got pregnant from her boyfriend and her life changed.

As the first African American to attend the all-girls Catholic school in her area, Hughes tried unsuccessfully to hide her pregnancy. She decided to take her life and choices into her own hands. Hughes married her boyfriend Alfred Liggins, Sr. just before she gave birth. After the birth of her son, she took life by the horns and never looked back.

More tough times came upon Hughes as her marriage unraveled after two years, leaving her a single parent. Despite the adversity, she defied the odds and graduated from high school. She later began working for KOWH a black owned radio station in Omaha, Nebraska. Hughes was great at what she did and began to catch the eye of other businesses.

She was offered and accepted a job as a lecturer at Howard University in the School of Communications. In 1973, Hughes became General Sales Manager at WHUR-FM, the radio station of Howard University. Her brilliance directly increased the stations revenue from $250,000 to $3 Million in one year.

Hughes was also the first African American woman to become Vice President and Manager of a radio station in Washington D.C. It was the imagination of Hughes that created the "quiet storm" format which black radio stations adopted and still use today. In 1980, Hughes and then husband Dewey Hughes purchased their own radio station, WOL-AM which would provide talk radio for African Americans in Washington D.C.

Because Hughes was a pioneer in the talk radio format for black owned stations, she endured her bumps and bruises. A learning process had begun. Hughes had to learn how to make a talk radio station in a population where it was not common. She also learned that talk radio is an expensive format. It cost her lots of money to stay afloat.

Around 1980, Hughes' station was located in an undesirable part of D.C. and her second marriage had come to an end. Hughes fell on tough times and was forced to live in her station with her son. She pressed on with her eyes on the prize refusing to be defeated. She was faced with a pivotal decision in her show format.

The bank that lent her the money to fund the station threatened to cut funding if she did not start playing music. In 1982, she changed her format to talk radio in the morning and music for the rest of the day. This move propelled her closer to her goal than she knew.

Without funds to pay a host for her morning talk radio, Hughes became the host and jettisoned herself into history. In 1986 WOL-AM turned its first profit, showing Hughes that she could have success if she worked hard enough for it. Hughes was able to purchase her second station WMMJ-FM in 1987. The sellers of the station sold it at an extremely high price, but she bought it anyway with persuasion from her son.

"Had we not been able to give WOL an FM big sister, we would not have survived"; stated Hughes. Her radio station eventually grew and became Radio One. She now owns over 70 stations in nine major U.S. markets. In 1999, Radio One became a publically traded company under the NASDAQ Stock Exchange.

In 2004, Hughes' Radio One launched TV One, a cable network for African Americans. Catherine Hughes is powering on still to this day as a media mogul and an inspiration to all. She is a person who started her dream with adversity. As a divorced teen mother, she was able to transform herself into a role model and a true giant. Mrs. Catherine Hughes, we stand on your shoulders.

Chapter 10:

Althea Gibson

Althea Gibson was born August 25, 1927 to parents Annie Bell and Daniel Gibson in Silver, South Carolina. As a young girl Gibson's life had its share of hardships. Her family eventually moved to Harlem, New York but still found hard times. Althea struggled in school and even skipped school altogether at times. But she found a love for ping pong which helped her regain focus. She began to get good at ping pong and even began winning tournaments sponsored by the local Harlem recreation department.

In 1941, she was introduced to the Harlem River Tennis Courts. This helped her develop a love for tennis. She began improving rapidly and in 1942, she won a tournament sponsored by the American Tennis Association. Althea also won the ATA title in 1944 and 1945. She lost the title in 1946, but went on to win the title consecutively from 1947 to 1956.

Because of her ATA success, Althea was offered a sports scholarship from Florida A&M University. Althea found herself struggling to get by as a black student. It was hard for her to get access to the tennis tournaments. In 1950, Alice Mable wrote an article in the *American Lawn Tennis* magazine, criticizing the sport of tennis for denying Gibson a chance to play in the major tournaments. Following the article, in 1951 Gibson was invited to Wimbledon, which made her the first African-American invited to the tournament.

In 1953, she became a top 10 player in the United States ranked as the No. 7 player in the United States. She also graduated from college that same year. Good fortune came Gibson's way in 1955 when she gained a sponsor in the United States Lawn Tennis Association. Because of her sponsor, she found herself on the State Department World Tour, taking her to India, Pakistan and Burma.

In 1956, Althea became the winner of the French Open. She won Wimbledon in 1957 and the U.S. Open in 1958. Gibson turned pro in 1959. Before she decided to become a professional tennis player, Gibson won 56 titles in single and doubles matches. One year after turning pro she won a singles title and began to profit from tennis for the first time.

Gibson being the gifted athlete, she tried her hand at golf and became the first African-American woman to compete on a pro golf tour. In 1958, Gibson returned to tennis on the newly created Open era, but found herself another victim of father time. Althea Gibson retired from tennis in 1971. Shortly after retirement, Gibson was inducted into the International Tennis Hall of Fame. Her life after tennis began with serving as the Commissioner of Athletics for the State of New Jersey, as well as a member of the Governor's Council on Physical Fitness.

Gibson's life after retirement later took a turn for the worse. She faced financial problems and bankruptcy, but friends stepped in and helped her maintain her lifestyle. Her health also began to fail her as heart problems and strokes took a toll on her aged body. In 2003, Althea Gibson died of respiratory failure.

Althea Gibson was a pioneer even thought she was too humble to except the honor. She broke ground in two sports; golf and tennis. She stared adversity in the eye and shined despite her challenges. Mrs. Althea Gibson we stand on your shoulders.

"A people without the knowledge of their past history, origin and culture is like a tree without roots."

Marcus Garvey

On the Shoulders of Giants: Volume 2. Central America

Coming Soon.......

Contact Us

www.Ontheshoulders1.com

Email:Ontheshoulders1@gmail.com

LIKE our On the Shoulders of Giants page

Follow us on Twitter & Instagram
@Ontheshoulders1

References

Mathieu Da Costa:
http://en.wikipedia.org/wiki/Mathieu_de_Costa,
http://www.blackhistorycanada.ca/events.php?id=21

Gaspar Yanga:
http://www.blackhistoryheroes.com/2011/05/gaspar-yanga-1570-african-slave-revolt.html,
http://en.wikipedia.org/wiki/Gaspar_Yanga,
http://www.blackpast.org/gah/yanga-gaspar-c-1545

Dr. Mae c. Jemison:
http://www.biography.com/people/mae-c-jemison-9542378#first-african-american-female-astronaut,
http://www.jsc.nasa.gov/Bios/htmlbios/jemison-mc.html, http://en.wikipedia.org/wiki/Mae_Jemison,
http://space.about.com/cs/formerastronauts/a/jemison
bio.htm

José Morelos y Pavon:
http://en.wikipedia.org/wiki/Jos%C3%A9_Mar%C3%A
Da_Morelos,
http://www.britannica.com/EBchecked/topic/392096/J
ose-Maria-Morelos

Bessie Coleman:
http://en.wikipedia.org/wiki/Bessie_Coleman,
http://womenshistory.about.com/od/aviationpilots/a/be
ssie_coleman.htm

Reginald F Lewis: Reginald F. Lewis, Blair S. Walker., "Why should white guys have all the fun?" Baltimore, Maryland., Black Classic Press, 1995. http://www.reginaldflewis.com/biography.php, http://en.wikipedia.org/wiki/Reginald_Lewis

Jovita Idár:
http://en.wikipedia.org/wiki/Jovita_Id%C3%A1r, http://persephonemagazine.com/2011/04/badass-ladies-of-history-jovita-idar/

Nathaniel Dett:
http://en.wikipedia.org/wiki/Robert_Nathaniel_Dett, http://lcweb2.loc.gov/diglib/ihas/loc.natlib.ihas.2000388 40/default.html

Catherine Hughes:
http://en.wikipedia.org/wiki/Cathy_Hughes, http://www.huffingtonpost.com/2012/08/17/catherine-hughes-radio-one_n_1798129.html

Althea Gibson:
http://en.wikipedia.org/wiki/Althea_Gibson, http://www.biography.com/people/althea-gibson-9310580